BUSINESS CENTS/SENSE

BUSINESS CENTS/SENSE

Caroline Munywoki

Copyright © 2020 by Caroline Munywoki.

ISBN:	Softcover	978-1-9845-8222-5
	eBook	978-1-9845-8221-8

All rights reserved. No part of this book may be reproduced or transmitted in any form or by any means, electronic or mechanical, including photocopying, recording, or by any information storage and retrieval system, without permission in writing from the copyright owner.

Any people depicted in stock imagery provided by Getty Images are models, and such images are being used for illustrative purposes only.
Certain stock imagery © Getty Images.

Print information available on the last page.

Rev. date: 06/03/2020

To order additional copies of this book, contact:
Xlibris
1-888-795-4274
www.Xlibris.com
Orders@Xlibris.com
811695

CONTENTS

Dedication vii
About the book ix

Chapter 1   Early to bed and early to Rise. 1
Chapter 2   Ideas to Action to Products and Services 5
Chapter 3   Taking Just Enough Time before Embarking On
            Your Business Venture 8
Chapter 4   Your 1, 2, 3 Business Plan 11
Chapter 5   What's In a Name? 14
Chapter 6   Pride, Respect, Confidence, Self-Discipline and
            Honesty for Success 17
Chapter 7   Separating Yourself from the Rest 23
Chapter 8   Education and Business - Introducing Practical
            Training and Business Cases early in Life to
            Invest in Human Capital. 26
Chapter 9   Tradition and culture affect how business is done
            globally 29
Chapter 10 The creative and Talented also need Business
            Education 32
Chapter 11 Building your empire from Cents 35
Chapter 12 The Power of Humility in Business Success -
            Humility and Customer Service in Business 38
Chapter 13 Mixed Voices and the impact they can have on
            diversified business success with the Conundrum
            around Romance 43
Chapter 14 Right Networks for Business Success 48
Chapter 15 Choosing the right management style at the right time ... 51

Chapter 16 Planning With Simple Budgeting Tools........................54
Chapter 17 Learning from failure, Destroying to Construct
            or Ripping off that rearview mirror...............................57
Chapter 18 Importance of Options, Imagination and
            Creativity rather than stressed upon Education........... 64
Chapter 19 It is never too late to have a smile on your face.............66
Chapter 20 Business Principles Derived from Nature always
            spell success 71

DEDICATION

To anyone dreaming of making it in their own world of Business and to my Nephews and Nieces who make my life worth living.

CHAPTER 1

Early to bed and early to Rise…..

"Early to bed and early to rise, makes someone healthy and wealthy and wise…"

Almost everyone at one point in their lives has sung this world renowned nursery rhyme – the implication that this rhyme has instilled to listeners is underestimated. Yet the notion that one will make it in business from following this particular line is but a fallacy.

Yes, following this rhyme will mostly give one good skin and a followed routine in whatever it is they do – making them a conditioned machine that will achieve what is laid out or have them thinking they are achieving by getting up every morning at a particular time and following a scheduled day log, with; lunch fixed at a particular time, snacks also fixed at specific times, meetings scheduled during perceived work hours and entertainment only enjoyed at scheduled times too.

Truth is – when in business, there is simply nothing like Early to Bed and Early to Rise. You work day and, or night. Optimal business persons actually work during wee hours of the night when the rest of the world is enjoying scheduled beauty naps.

A quite successful young man that I know of who lives in Las Vegas, Nevada - USA is doing quite well for someone his age – this young man has a wife, a great big house close to the strip with an impressive swimming pool. His wife is a Registered Nurse Assistant and they only get to see each other a couple of hours each on work days. The young man never gets up during the day – he is completely nocturnal. He gets home at around 6 am most mornings and sleeps till late in the afternoon - he has created his own kind of play list and picked the right place to practice his skill and make a sustained profit from his art.

He mixes his own house music in great clubs and he might never run out of gigs, as, he is not like the normal Disc Jockeys (DJ's) – he has used technology to revolutionize his art and uses it effectively and creatively to WoW his clients.

He has cleverly designed outfits when mixing his music, like glowing teeth (Bling Bling Grills), glowing hats, bracelets, glow in the dark skeleton outfits and they change color with the beat of every song in his music collection. His music is not only energetic, engaging and extremely catchy – but watching him play it is entertaining on its own; Sort of like having two shows in one; hence, he gets paid really well to perform.

This makes him a wanted man in the crazy Las Vegas night life – Does he follow the "early to bed and early to rise…" nursery rhyme? No.

Is he successful – unquestionably so. Is he a business minded lad? Most definitely; does he work hard? Undoubtedly!

Finding what was being done before and following without questioning whether things can be done differently to accommodate business success from different thinking can hold most back.

Schedules are good, timing even better, but if you feel lethargic every time you get up in the morning to follow your schedule? Something is amiss. Sometimes nursery rhymes are there to give our children moral direction – but when we get older and recognize they were written with the intention to give guidance and hope to young minds – then we can alter them to realize better business success.

Early to bed and early to rise, will most definitely make you healthier – but wealthier will be something that will come from more than just that.

Some of the main reasons people get into Business are for financial freedom and independence and the joy of being your own boss – the extra perks and bonuses that come with it are a myriad – especially when your venture gets to the point where you can now afford to get a few more people on board.

Not only would you be bringing blessings your way from the universe, you will also be providing a service that is an outcry around the globe – Unemployment!

Your employees now become your number one asset and their output, work environment and motivation will lie solely on you. Not only do you have to know each one of them on a personal basis it will help if you work around their schedules to get maximum profit from the very talented and hardworking employees.

No matter what business you are in; services or products – you can always choose to think outside the tin can to get the maximum from your employees and ensure their happiness – because we all know, - happy employees mean better profit margins.

You might want to shift or alter your working hours to beat the dreaded traffic; this can be done in whatever part of the globe your business is. You can schedule a strategic meeting after, and only after, you have identified the employees with whom you want to work with (you cannot afford to do this with just anyone who presents you with an impressive resume, nor a relative or an in-law – you have to make sure that employees given this amazing opportunity have to have earned it) Work with them for a given amount of time – take your time to learn them – sometimes it takes months to know how an individual works, give them test runs or assignments on a whim, if they deliver within the agreed upon time frame, then make a mental check of that, keep giving assignments here and there to see if the employee will come through – if you are let down more than thrice, especially on timelines and tasks – let go completely – that is not an employee worth keeping; if, they will not deliver on assignments and timelines as promised on the very first days of struggle – chances are when you get nicer they will walk all over you.

It is better to let go early than wait for years only to hurt much more than if you had done it after seeing the signs.

Once you have identified your true employees and learnt some of their habits, you can now work around "early to bed and early to rise". Remember it is your personal business and your business is like your child; if you spare the rod you will spoil the child. The early years will be very shaky and difficult but consistent discipline, planning and maybe, even some tears will only make the future much better and solidly sustainable for you.

At the strategic meeting, set the schedule yourself under guidance from other employees or partners and extensive research on alternative work schedules on reaping maximum profit. You now have the power to set your timeline and you can assign duties based on hourly rates, timed tasks and mostly the characteristics of your employees. When the employee feels some sort of autonomy, they will work much better. Please note that your bottom line is your profit and sustainability so duties delivered only means a win-win for you and your employees.

Make your employees feel empowered like the Las Vegas nocturnal DJ, this will only bring in smiles for you and the future of your venture.

Once you have covered and fully understood the "early to bed and early to rise" rhyme, you have actually killed 3 birds with one stone. You have shown the business world that you can alter your working hours, work around the Global clock with very little manpower and your clients can reach you at any time and the best part about it – you are learning; and in more ways than one, teaching your employees how to work smarter instead of harder.

CHAPTER 2

Ideas to Action to Products and Services

I like observing people in busy areas. I like to sit in a restaurant, bar, side corner of a busy street or in a party and just observe. I find it interesting how people act differently when they know someone is watching. I have sat at off road benches where tea is being served and kiosks where 'Khat' is being sold or chewed. I also like visiting the slums in Africa. To me, these are the places you will find honest people who say what they really feel and indulge you in insightful business and life conversations.

I am usually the one to introduce businesses and sustainability into the conversation, as 95% of the time someone will have something to talk about. I cannot over emphasize how many times I have heard of great ideas.

One guy, I call him Mungai, who lives in slum near a town called Kamukunji – Nairobi, has quite the plethora. He usually talks much when he has had some alcohol or is chewing 'Khat'. If I wrote down every single idea this guy has come up with, I would have a 500 page book and it would probably be titled 'A million business ideas' sadly his ideas, as brilliant as they are, remain just that – Ideas.

Ideas are from simple farming techniques to solar powered plants that he has designed, to machines that interpret dreams and high security technology gadgets.

Mungai is the "one" who thought up of the pressure washer; he is convinced that if he had put his idea on paper, all the pressure washers would be paying him a dividend for his invention. He is also the "one" who thought of the finger print security device; yet again, he is so sure he would have been rubbing shoulders with Bill Gates if only; he had worked on his idea.

Just the other day, Mungai told me he had the answer to end hunger in the world; he exclaimed, he had had a week of sleepless nights stewing over this 'one' idea - a single pill made from natural products that will suppress the hunger feeling subsequently imitating food satisfaction. I think this idea is phenomenal. I would love to get such the pill. In fact, I would pay for such the pill. With it, I would not need to worry about cooking, washing dishes, and would have an extra 3 hours in my day to work instead of preparing a meal and sitting down to enjoy it.

In the world of entrepreneurship, brilliant ideas are plentiful; Great execution, hardly much. In his new book – Making Ideas Happen: Overcoming the obstacles between vision and reality; Edison said it best: "Genius is one percent inspiration, ninety-nine percent perspiration."

Innovative and creative ideas are at the heart of most successful businesses. Ideas by themselves, however, have little value. They need to be developed, turned into innovative products or services and commercialized successfully so as to enable you to reap the benefits of your innovation and creativity.

Mungai, just like many entrepreneurs needs to start acting and spare the empty talk for bystanders or people like me, who like to listen. But if he truly wants to establish a business and work on 'that' idea that cannot get out of his mind then he must think about adhering to some handy tips.

He could first start by reducing his main projects (those that are very dear to him) into components and create reasonable and achievable steps that will move him forward. He might also want to generate his ideas into moderation – knowing what you can and cannot do is paramount and new ideas will often get you off track. The challenge would be to balance idea generation and relentless focus. He might even consider acting without conviction – as opposed to what we have been taught – to think before we act; in Mungai's case waiting builds apathy and increases the chances that another genius idea will capture his fancy, enthusiasm and energy.

Finally, if the idea still lingers, Mungai might want to check out his competitors, sometimes visiting your competitor's business premise and seeing what they are doing can be a powerful force for actualization and implementation.

CHAPTER 3

Taking Just Enough Time before Embarking On Your Business Venture

My first question at the beginning of any business class is? What are you looking for in life and out of this class? And the most common and unanimous answer is Financial Freedom and more money than can be spent. Great – but how much is one willing to do to achieve this?

I was thrilled when a friend of mine told me she was opening a video library in the heart of Nairobi – What's your niche? I asked and what will be the core of your business? She had a brilliant idea of online movie rentals – using the same business strategy Netflix used to launch their product. She also said that no-one else is doing that in Kenya and I was very happy for her. She had already setup internet services and had the computers to accomplish the mission. So my main concern was the money – how much will it take to be self-sustaining and after how long will she start reaping profits?

Her charges were not that high and since the postal services in Kenya did not offer a flat rate for mailing packages – the clients would pay for the postage. She was also not going to lock her clients into a monthly subscription and I thought this was a perfect concept as she would not have to worry about running her business on credit or chasing payments and additionally having to create a system that makes sure your clients remain behind your bars.

I encouraged her and told her to mentally prepare herself for unforeseen or unanticipated businesses operational problems as I was not very conversant with that kind of business.

Months later I came back home to Kenya and since I love watching movies a friend took me to the city centre to buy some movies – initially, I was amazed at being able to buy movies at very many places in town – secondly and most importantly a movie was only 50Kshs i.e less than a US dollar. My jaw dropped – how can I purchase a clear movie for only 50Kshs?

I quickly started to re-think my friends business model – would she actually have clientele if simple business math was applied? Most likely not

Facts: Buying a movie in town on your lunch break or after work will only cost you 50Kshs. The convenience of ordering from the comfort of your house is appealing but it will cost you more than 50Kshs to pay for postage and you will have to wait a few days before you can enjoy your movies. A business model like this would work well in the first world countries – but if it had to work in Kenya the target market would have to be the upper class and the business office would probably work well in those and certain parts of the country. It might also target customers that enjoy the clarity of Blu-ray discs and we all know not a big percentage of Kenyans have Blu-ray capable viewing electronics.

If my friend had also carefully studied the Netflix model and how they have been struggling financially in the past years – she would probably have decided to alter her business strategy. Netflix provides a monthly flat rate service for the rental of movies and the clients create an ordered list - which lets them rent more than 2 movies at a time and once they mail those back they can rent more – they have different tiers for different movie lovers and the more you can pay determines the number of movies and service Netflix provides. Great Concept, great model and attractive to a wider target market – unfortunately Netflix's business model did not work that well, not for a long period of time – they started going through trying times and started coming up with different ways to attract and keep their clientele. They tried everything I could think possible as per concerning increasing profit – from international expansion, to streaming online movies, to changing names and revising their packages and prices – but it is simply a rough market and they have mastered it on other channels and almost stopped shipping movies in the mail box.

A closer look at Netflix's numerous and failed attempts to save that business model of mail-ins from my friend might have saved her some operational issues – I am not sure how her business is doing – but I would imagine it must be tougher than she had imagined – Kenya's structure and market will not be good to her neither will it embrace her brilliant idea or concept.

Carrying out business in different parts of the world really varies when it comes to very small and sometimes not even considered factors as taught in most business schools.

The importance of a thorough market analysis and taking into consideration factors that seem trivial but of substantial consequence to business like cultural differences, economic environment and stiff competition is of utter importance especially when embarking on a new venture, product or service in a new market.

Doing your homework diligently for your business while you evolve, will not only save you some headaches, but will always show in the results.

CHAPTER 4

Your 1, 2, 3 Business Plan

One of my entrepreneurship skills class session entails the students write a brief business plan with intent to what business they plan to venture into. Most of the students use the internet to come up with ways into which they will work on their preferred businesses. A big percentage of the documentation they use from the internet gives a good read – but what they do not understand is that you cannot use someone else's business plan in some other region of the world to fully execute your own business.

Business concepts remain the same universally but execution and sustainability differ depending on your environment and market.

Most of my students' business plans have glorified projections and their market analysis clearly depicts great profit. In short, one look at the business plan will tell you that some issues have yet to be thought of. For example Competition, Risk, Challenges and so forth.

I tend to think that before you embark on your venture you should draft at least 3 business plans.

Your own individual Business Plan:

This plan is the truest of them all. I refer to it as the naked business plan. It covers almost everything including the risk of failure.

No business life lesson can be complete without a discussion on risks and risk management and No Business can be started without embracing Risk. Risks are inherent in everything we do - Business risk management is the key to ensure risks are identified and a plan-B or C thought of. Some risks we can control while others we cannot.

This plan should cover who you are as an individual, what your honest strengths are, your weaknesses, and different follow up plans lest your venture does not go as planned. It should clearly address questions like;- Can you persevere through tough times? Do you have a strong desire to be your own boss? Do the judgments you make in life regularly turn out well? Do you have an ability to conceptualize the whole of a business? Do you possess the high level of energy, sustainable over long hours, to make a business successful? Do you have significant specialized business experience?

The financial projections in this plan should cover in the very least 5 different modules. This must be the plan that you read out at night and you work on yourself as an individual to get prepared for anything.

Business Plan for investors:

I like to call this the headlines business plan. You only have one shot at getting investors so make the best out of it. This is the plan that shows what team you will be working with and how you plan to invest to make money for your investors. This one needs to show a well laid out plan that shows short and long term financial gain.

The confidence coupled with experience shown in this document is what will determine whether you will get the initial investment you seek. Confident business men and women feel competent from the inside out. They use their knowledge and talents to genuinely try to be useful and succeed at hand. Truth is, to succeed in business – having and proving Self- Confidence on your plan is vital. Most investors will always often than not work with successful business men and women that have some level of confidence.

The financial projections in this case can be 3 or 5 year term and do not need to have different modules. They are there to show profit.

But you cannot glorify it too much nor try and get a lot of money for the start up. You must mention what your competition is and how you plan on separating yourself from the rest with your own niche market – having a business plan that does not have a thorough SWOT analysis could raise a red flag and you might end up not getting anyone to invest in your venture.

There are many reasons that startups or businesses fail and some entrepreneurs could be in denial when dealing with their own ideas and concepts. Pick the right team, get professional advice, try separate yourself from the rest - in order to achieve your own niche, do not spend too much money – most people think that having a lot of money is fundamental in doing business; that, is but a fallacy – you can make much out of very little.

The last one is the Universal Business Plan:

This is the plan that you started out with – the one you did sitting research to come up with pros and cons. The plan that has been developed from different internet searches to better understand what you will be dealing with. This is the longest and truthfully the "wannabe" business plan. It lets you see how things have been done differently and gives ideas into working with your naked business plan. This one has a lot of information and as you keep self- actualizing you tend to sieve out information or material that is irrelevant for your business.

Without this one – it is very hard to cover everything that needs to be covered with your proposed venture.

Starting a business is not for everyone, but great planning will always show in the results.

CHAPTER 5

What's In a Name?

Last year I travelled a lot to Wamunyu, Machakos County -Kenya. I always made a pit stop in Machakos town to buy the best samosas I have ever tasted in a restaurant called T-Tot. Just before T-tot, there is a center called "Susu Center" – I have no idea what they do in there but I gather it is some sort of professional institute with some learning facilities.

To the best of my knowledge, Susu is not an English word; although there is a University in South Hampton that has a Student's Union whose acronyms spell SUSU. What I know, is that this name subtly resonates a sheepish smile to my face every time I drive by that center.

Choosing a business name is as vital and as crucial as writing a realistic business plan. Your business name will say what you do, who you are and can be a very strong advertising element of your business that may eventually be used for strategic branding.

A simple business name can make or break your business. The name can literally determine how far your company will go with the endeavor.

I personally love Sushi, but one of the funniest Sushi business names I have come across was FUKU Sushi. I think they had great Sushi but their name no matter what it meant to the owners might spell a few mistakes and loose them some customers in America.

Another strange example was a funeral home, where the owners surname was Slaughter. He named his company "Slaughter and Son

Funeral directors". No matter how tempting or self-conceited it might be to use your family name on your business, sometimes the name just does not go well with your chosen profession.

I tried to dabble my hands into the Bar and Restaurant business at one point in my confused life and the only thing I knew was that I would never have called that bar Munywokis – this is because in my Kamba tribe the name means "the one who drinks alcohol or honey" and that could have spelled - an alcoholic selling alcohol, which might absolutely killed the Bar's long term success.

There are so many ways of being creative with business names – if you lack the creativity, why not try going with words that literally have meaning and are related to what you are trying to achieve from the venture.

Like Michael Jackson's "Never – Never Ranch" which must have come from Never Never Land - a noun, that actually means, an idealized imaginary place where everything is perfect.

Or if you are looking to just be exceptional by separating yourself from the rest; then you can try using unique words; for example, words having all the vowels (a e i o u) once and only once and in order. Like – abstemious, anemious, facetious or caesious, and have usable meanings.

If completely lost and lack some source of creativity, then you can use the simplest way of picking a business name and use the location of your premise to identify the business. Like; Finnlines Shipping, American Airlines, Nairobi Hospital, Machakos Hardware, Davis Sports and Goods, Oregon Flowers, Crédit Foncier de France, Bank of Moscow and so forth.

Humor and a comedic play on words can be a great way to catch some attention and smiles from passers-by. And customers can also be funny. What one group finds amusing, another can find distasteful; One has to be careful not to overdo it like "Manlove Dental Practice" or "BBQ Tanning Beds" as this can elicit bad tastes in future clientele and ruin your business instead of achieving smiles and profit.

The importance of taking into consideration many factors before picking that one name cannot be under emphasized. That name might as well be the first thing that pulls clients and or customers in, itself.

Customers should be drawn to a name that not only stands out from your competition, but is also trustworthy and highly professional.

Business names are like first impressions. That is the first thing your potential customers will notice and will make instant judgments, on where and whom they want to associate with and put their money.

Getting a good balance for a name between simple, lasting and trustworthy is not as easy as it sounds – as this is the first thing you have to decide upon prior to launch; therefore it is of utter importance that you strike the right tone for your business.

Consider the following before you pick a name that you might regret later;

1. Research as much as you can - talk to trusted friends, family and carry out internet research.
2. Pick a name that can allow for possible future business development and one that will have a suitable acronym associated with it that can be used for Branding
3. Keep it simple with a niche unique to your business.

The payoff for choosing the right business name will always show in the results.

CHAPTER 6

Pride, Respect, Confidence, Self-Discipline and Honesty for Success

During an Executive Masters in Business Administration (EMBA) Session on International business expansion the words hub and spoke came up. It was apparent that not all participants were very well conversant with the Hub and spoke business model. The lecturer from Netherlands explained it quite fast as if the participants knew what he was talking about but I felt the topic needed more discussion – I wanted to get up and explain it in very simple terms giving simple examples but to my surprise, I froze. I got cold feet.

I was lucky to be invited to a 'Training for Trainers' (TOT) and was in the Financial Module of the program; I met very interesting and learned folk for that one week – I got to engage in a great Financial Group and we came up with different ideas of how a Financial Training Module should be organized. During our lunch breaks I made sure to sit with different people just so I could diversify my learning portfolio and get to learn as much as I could from this diverse group of people. Break time discussions were exciting – most of everyone there is specialized and very knowledgeable in their fields – but this was not shown during the learning sessions.

A good friend was explaining a great business concept while mixing it with his own personal life and the challenges he has faced in business and life as a whole – his remarks were exemplary and his comments on how business should be run were fantastic – but he was very hesitant and somewhat pessimistic when it came to him seeing a brighter business future. He was a little bit pensive into exploring his own idea and he hit the nail on the head when he muttered – business and his life would be much different if he worked on his confidence.

Spot on!

The reason I got cold feet during the EMBA session was because I did not believe in myself at that particular moment and my confidence level at that time was questionably low. I had the knowledge, knew exactly how I would explain it in simple terms – but I just did not do it.

The reason I was saddened at some presentations and discussions from the TOT program was because no matter how learned and sharp most of my colleagues were, they showed very little in their own ability; especially when it came to the full class discussions.

I tend to believe that there is a very big difference between confidence and arrogance – I do not like arrogant people and I feel arrogance stems from some sort of insecurity where an arrogant person wants to feel smart at the expense of the other feeling stupid – arrogant people will correct simple flaws like grammatical errors and make them a huge deal in order to get unnecessary attention and make the other person feel of a lesser kind.

Confident business men and women feel competent from the inside out. They use their knowledge and talents to genuinely try to be useful and succeed at hand. Some arrogant people might be smarter or more skilled than confident people but it is confidence that is most likely to see one succeed in business than blatant disrespectful arrogance.

Truth is, to succeed in business – having Self-Confidence is vital. Most successful business men and women have some level of confidence; yet there are days, minutes, hours or weeks in the business person's life when they are unsure of how to tackle some business challenges- everyone at one time goes through these shaky times – but the trick is to stay on track and not let a trying time hold you back to achieving business success.

Learning how to overcome bouts of self-doubt can only come from within. One must be completely honest with themselves by assessing ones' ability and deficiencies and get comfortable enough to work on them and assertively correct them. You have to practice doing things that you have not done before and could be unsure of and embracing new opportunities to prove to yourself and others that you can confront and work on difficult things.

One important factor to always remember is that your confidence must bear exemplary and evident results – one must be able to deliver on their confidence making sure it's quality, memorable and sustainable results.

It is easy to think that most people are confident because of their success but the truth is most people achieve their success through confidence. Individuals who have unfaltering confidence and use sustainable business practices will always show in the results.

To survive in today's merciless business world, one has to take pride in what they sell. Quality in business is very important and is undoubtedly easy to define. Everyone wants quality that is appropriate to the price they are willing to pay and the level of competition in the market.

Whatever business you're in, good quality will help you determine your success. This will ensure customer loyalty, a great brand reputation, attracting and retaining clients and most importantly a great referral program.

It's simple, if you are not proud in your business to begin with; you are deciding to begin to fail. Just like work, if you are not proud of what you're doing, chances are – you are not staying there that long.

If you do not believe in yourself, your business will not flourish. One characteristic that successful people have is that they believe in themselves and in most of what they do. You have to mentally prepare yourself to battle any obstacles that you will encounter in achieving your goals. You have to portray what is inside outside. In some countries' business owners, business isn't business; it's personal. Before starting a business most people are thinking- to gain independence, for flexibility, a sense of autonomy and a great sense of pride. That pride should be clearly evident in the products you sell. If you would not buy that product at the price you are selling it – then, you need to rethink your marketing strategy.

Firms, as well, need to incorporate quality management into their organizational structure to succeed and have to work hard to retain and improve their reputation for great quality which can easily be tarnished by a story in the news about quality failure. Corporations who treat their staff with pride will surely reap great result; and could adopt a quality program to assess good design in the looks and style; if the product or service is functional; if it is durable and has good value for money, consistently – to ensure overall quality.

Taking pride in who you are and what you do will ensure quality success. That prides' payoff will always show in the results!

I met a savvy 'businessman' late last year. I had the opportunity to interact with him at length. As expected he had a good mouth on him – so I had initially assumed he must have started in sales then talked, hustled and worked his way up to other businesses like real estate, food industry and supplies.

He was very well dressed, keeps up with fashion trends from all over the world and can talk to anyone – this man can literally sell snow to Eskimos. I was at awe every time he opened his mouth as I learnt something each time. Surprisingly I had/have never visited his business premise – he had taken me around different businesses but mostly his friends or families.

So, I decided to ask for a tour to one of his place of business – I was interested to see just how one of his many businesses runs and how he has organized its operation and structure; so that I can share working and practical examples with my students in one of my classes.

There was nothing.

The 'businessman' was and still is living in a fantasy world – he has literally taken years to learn how to run businesses and helped grow some businesses but has never done anything for himself.

He has not come to terms with whom he is and is clearly struggling to keep up with the charade that has taken years to build around his friends and all the people around him.

Psychologists would refer to this man's condition as mythomania; A man suffering from Pseudologia fantastica. But, in simple business terms he would be a great confident man – if the term fake it till you make it is true then this 'businessman' has out-lived it – the making it, has not, will not, and is just not happening.

He has managed to continually falsify everything to no discernible end in view, from simple to extensive and very complicated issues and this has manifested over a very long period of years and might last his lifetime.

All business persons know that the notions of business and honesty don't always go hand in hand. The term honesty sounds so basic yet is a vital cornerstone of whether you shall make it in business or not. Warren Buffet could not have said it louder "Trust is like the air we breathe. When it's present nobody really notices. But when it's absent, everybody notices"

When starting a business – the first thing one should be clear about is who they are. Honesty with one self;

If you are unsure of the person you are – chances are you will be unsure of what you really want for your business and how you will successfully achieve it.

Subsequently one must know that his customers or clients will require clean and honest business – no matter what business it is that one is in.

Honesty with others;

Fool one man – no problem, but fool the whole community and chances are you are not going too far with your business.

Lastly, to succeed one must be honest with his business – some entrepreneur stories are too meticulous. They can talk anyone into thinking they are lying in a bed of roses so much so that they start to believe in their own lies and do not come to the real terms that their business is just not succeeding.

When business persons practice the term "Honesty is the best policy" and do not just use it as a wall placard it shows. Entrepreneurship and Business is like life itself; morals and ethics must be practiced to do well in business and succeed. The value of honesty in business is just like in life – it has obvious and subtle implications, with dire consequences.

Honest business practices should be applied in all facets of one's business and in every situation. Honesty will build a strong foundation of trust with peers, competition, employees and separate you from the rest.

The payoff in how honest you are and the ethics you practice will always show in the open

CHAPTER 7

Separating Yourself from the Rest

One of my jobs I had when I was pursuing my Masters degree was a janitor at that college. Yes, a cleaner. I did not like it as much as I liked my colleagues, but it paid part of my tuition and I needed it – so I had to be proud of it and I did it well. I hated the fact that I slept past midnight and had to wake up at 4 in the morning just to go and clean as my shift was from 5a.m to 8.am.

My Janitorial supervisor (Rocky) was great at his job and a perfectionist; he gave attention to every detail. We all had shifts that were well documented and well explained making him an impeccable planner. For instance, If you were not going to show up for work in case of any illness or some sort of emergency he asked that you call or notify him not less than 8 hours in advance and if you do not communicate – your pay is docked for that day. Strict?, Yes, - but with completely valid business reasons.

My janitorial supervisor played a huge role in the college's strategic planning committee and I will tell you why below.

I visited quite a busy office building a few months ago at around 10.30 a.m. and I opted for the stairs instead of the elevator as I was in one of those rare fitness moods. To my surprise I had to walk along the edge as that was the time the building was being cleaned. I was floored. I courteously asked one of the cleaners if their manager or caretaker was around and they said he is never there. The staircase was messy with soap. And traffic from muddy shoes looked like the janitors were there to throw mud balls instead of clean.

I asked what time their first shift was and they said at 10.00.am

When one decides to start a business in cleaning they have to know that working hours will vary from other normal working hours.

For instance, the thorough cleaning can be done early in the morning before traffic starts building up in the office – regular spot checks can be done once every two hours with managerial supervision and lastly if the weather is not that great – placemats can be put in strategic areas to curb mess coming in from the outside.

Rocky – was in charge of the entire campus and he knew every tiny little nook of that building. When I got on board – Rocky personally trained me – from cleaning the toilets, wiping the windows, changing toilet rolls, mopping the floor, waxing, dusting, to taking out the garbage and sorting out the recycling bins. He did this with every employee in order to assure that none of the employees would ever come back and say they did not know what to do and how to do it – Hence instilling employee accountability.

Rocky used a very simple word document that he used to track the hours, supplies and toiletries used per shift, time taken on specific tasks and attendance of his employees.

From this document – Rocky could tell you how much hand soap would be used in Lab 5 next week as opposed to Lab 8 – He had kept this document for the 5 years he had worked there and as simple as it was – it was more than effective and downright perfect. The data he had collected on that sheet – was worth millions to the college and his input and knowledge invaluable, especially when it came to budgeting.

Although they do not eat at the same restaurants, Rocky's knowledge at annual strategic planning meetings is priceless. Rocky kept that huge college impeccably clean, he had a great attitude, drove to succeed, was not ashamed to get his hands dirty, and although he was not liked by most he was highly respected. He used his basic educational skills and turned this into effective technical knowledge.

That college was one of the cleanest colleges I have been to and top management valued Rocky's work and input to the extent that they used it in their annual strategic and financial planning.

It really does not bear much substance what job you are in or what title you have or your physical appearance - when you separate yourself from the rest and it is result evident, it is very hard to bury the truth and business numbers will never lie. You shall positively and increasingly advance towards your business goals.

Your personal business sense understanding and approach will always show in the results.

CHAPTER 8

Education and Business - Introducing Practical Training and Business Cases early in Life to Invest in Human Capital.

One of my favorite past times is sitting in the park, playing and watching kids play. It is amazing how you can tell so much about a child just from watching how he/she is playing and how they interact with other children.

The most amazing about these little angels is the ability to have a sponge as a brain – whatever they learn they keep for a really long time, sometimes even their entire lives. The early years of the child could be the most impactful on how that child will lead his adult life.

Business is a lot like Art – some are born with the talent – but others teach themselves and work at getting better. The results of the training always show with time.

The importance of grooming our youth and children on business early in life cannot be over emphasized. Developed countries have embraced this and come up with national strategies to foster this into their young and growing population

April 26th and November 7th have been marked the day to bring your child to work in the US and in Canada respectively. Great national concept and fosters some sense of family cohesion. Ultimately we all need to learn from working examples and come up with a sustainable, financially sensible manner of introducing business and business thinking into our children's lives.

Business concepts are universal – but how you do your business in different environments and markets differs and this stems from a number of things – tradition, technology, exposure and practical training.

As the ministries and departments of Education around the Globe continuously revise the curriculum they should consider integrating business learning with practical real case studies into childhood learning specifically in Primary or early years of school. Revising the curriculum and having knowledgeable instructors create an early investment in workforce development would benefit future leaders financially in years to come. High Quality Childhood education is healthy development; environments and experiences in early years are very influential in the development of a child's brain.

James Heckman, a professor of economics at the University of Chicago, researched and proved that the quality of childhood development heavily influences economic and social outcomes for individuals and society at large. Great economic gains can be had by investing in early business and basic financial education. According to Heckman, the Rates of Return to human capital investment vary at different ages. By integrating financial and business classes geared appropriately towards specific age groups then, we can harness 4 core integral and economically viable gains.

Investing in early financial and business education will provide equal access to successful early and recognizable human development.

Developing and nurturing of cognitive, business and financial skills in young adults.

Sustainability - Early business sense and development with effective mandatory education through to adulthood and parenthood.

Gain: Educated, Skilled, Capable, Productive, Valuable, Effective workforce globally that will pay dividends for generations to come.

To reap maximum profit and offer great promise, this has to be a joint effort between parents, teachers, and the community as a whole and will surely be a rewarding area of influence for the Business Segment. Every sector of society has a stake in a child's future and must be active partners for our future financial success. Introducing Early Financial and Business education in our primary schools is not only a smart investment with positive returns, but the most prudent thing to do.

Parents and Community should not encourage "wannabe hustlers", incompetent workers and or uneducated businessmen. We must improve on our standards of living and have these policies considered with the economic development plans.

The Return on practical business training and knowledge is clear and the earlier this intervention occurs the greater the Payoff.

CHAPTER 9

Tradition and culture affect how business is done globally

Death and the mourning ceremonies thereafter are practiced very differently in different parts of the world.

A prominent politician and patriot in Kenya passed away about a year ago. His name was Martin Oyondi Shikuku. His arrangements caused some controversy and were considered highly nontraditional as Shikuku had planned the pre-digging of his own grave and had laid out how the funeral and subsequent proceedings would go.

It was not normal especially in his culture for someone to pre-dig a grave, and make arrangements for his funeral while still alive.

Sometimes tradition as deep rooted as they are can affect the way business is carried out in a modern perspective

This particular funeral could be used as a case study in a Financial Planning or Financial Management Graduate Level Course.

Allow me to extrapolate 5 financially solid reasons from a simple business perspective:

1. It takes us away from some tying and binding traditional ways of thinking that may not be applicable in today's business world. Pre-digging a grave is not a taboo. Coming to terms with your immortality is noble and planning for it, simply prudent.

Additionally, since embalming is not required for the first 24 hours; one will most definitely save on the mortuary and embalming expenses. Using Shikuku as a case study especially in an African context will allow for business schools to introduce a different way of thinking in our future financial and business leaders or business persons running business in Africa

2. Financial Planning - putting your financial affairs in order; writing a will, sharing your bank accounts, title deeds, insurance policies, mortgages, birth certificates, death certificates, any kind of financial verbal agreements with your loved ones as well as a trusted lawyer. Making a list of all your possessions will save your family having to search through piles of papers to find the information they need, at a time of great stress.

Organized and well written or verbally shared instructions on these documents will surely take the hustle off people running around frantically trying to put your funeral together

3. Shikuku Proclaimed in public that he did not wish his family or loved ones to go through financial difficulties after his demise; should be a point worth mentioning and noting - chances are, that no distant relatives or friends will appear claiming they had left assets or collectables from the deceased.

This ensures that life for his heirs and heiresses may go on more swiftly financially with a number of people as key witnesses of the deceased spoken words.

4. Accepting death and putting some good business humor in it. Writing your own obituary and picking your own picture, and maybe even designing your coffin to suit what you love most. I have seen some coffins shaped and designed like cell phones, others like angels, and some like beer bottles. Preparing all this will save you lots of time and we all know time is money.

Passing on is inevitable, it does not hurt to have some humor around it or design a funeral that you would want before your demise.

5. If you have not written down your bucket list or do not intend to write one – you might want to consider working on a financial bucket list. We all have a secret list of things we really want to do in our lifetime. If you are nearing the end of your life, you clearly don't have as much time to accomplish this list before you "kick the bucket." Start today and do what you can. If you are not imminently facing the end of your life, make your list and start working on it now. Starting now will allow you to accomplish more than you ever thought possible, rather than rushing around at a later point in life, when you have limited time.

You can compare this to an adjustable business plan that will govern the rest of your financial life. The list can include; how much you want to contribute towards your retirement, whether or not you will have pre-dug graves for your spouse or spouses, shapes of your graves, consider if you would be cremated and your ashes made into a pencil that can be used draw your portrait or whatever it is that tickles your fancy.

The truth is we shall all die; unexpectedly or not - but how you plan your finances by preparing for your own death in advance shall relieve the decision-making burden and financial constraint on those whom we love and create the opportunity for a peace-filled end of life. The mere reason Certified Financial Planners exist and will continue to be in demand.

May, Martin Oyondi Shikuku Rest In Eternal Peace and the lessons learnt from a brave, charismatic patriot live in the minds of Africans for a long time.

CHAPTER 10

The creative and Talented also need Business Education

I do not watch TV much but some of my favourite entertainment talent shows are the Kenyan "Tusker Project Fame" "American Idol", "Britain's got talent" or "So you think you can dance". These shows are an indication of how this world is filled with people of great and different talent all coming in different shapes and sizes.

I was proud to read about how the Kenyan Ruth Matete stole the show and is taking home KShs 5 million in cash. I sat back and thought to myself what a lucky young girl and how proud her family must be especially since she has come from a humble background. I also thought – I hope she a mentor to advise her on how to make the most of that 5 million – because, only the gods know when she will ever hold such kind of money in her hands again.

Fact is many a talented folk have fallen short of good financial advice and gone from soaring to flooring in their mint. The emphasis on basic business education or sustainable business projects have not been a concern to celebrities or talented persons up until the money goes flush.

Remember, MC Hammer? – Well, he couldn't touch his own house after making a killing from his album. He could not even afford to stay in the 30 million dollar mansion he had bought and could not afford to keep his 200-person entourage after very few months of fame and literally swimming in lots of cash. He had to file for bankruptcy and collect the pieces. If he had taken basic business classes or sought financial advice from experts he would be well sustained and might probably never have to go back to the studio to try and whisk some magic into producing a second album as untouchable as the first. Celebrities that have made such mistakes are a myriad – likes of Cindy Lauper, Kellis and Chris Tucker. Another good example is Mike Tyson – he earned almost 300 Million dollars in his career and ended up having to file for bankruptcy owing 27 million. Why? Ludicrous investments, lavish living, and most importantly lack of sound business advice and poor financial investments. All these celebrities thankfully have bounced back and might soar even further than they first started, but now, wiser.

Business and Financial tutors should use real examples like these in their classes to educate their students on the importance of well-rounded business education. The number of talented youth and adults I have met is staggering and what they have in common is that they are all or mostly struggling with sustaining their finances.

The questions that linger in my mind and material I would like to read; would be a follow up on local talent show from previous winners. What did they do with their loot? Where they are now and most importantly are they financially stable? What lessons can be shared to budding talents or artists on financial management?

Yes you have talent, yes you can dance and yes you are beautiful, but can your God Given gift sustain your lifestyle and have you the basic business sense to know that you need to make essential and important business decisions?

The importance of basic business courses is unquestionable and the advantages a myriad. Business education will provide you with a plethora of courses and plenty of skills needed for success in business. And if you are too busy working in the studio – then it would benefit you greatly to seek expert financial advice way in advance. I am not talking about calling a rich relative or friend to come over and discuss business – a trained expert that will look at options from different angles and advice on what you can or cannot delve in today's business world.

Talented individuals have a natural advantage over the common citizen in business as successful entrepreneurs are highly creative. Unfortunately success as an artist is not just about talent or whom you rub shoulders with. There is no magic formula and you need to consider sustainable business options to thrive in business using your talent. One has to open up their talent for business success, and integrate talent with business management.

Undeniably artistic creative talent is important and should also be about creative entrepreneurial Talent. Talents across the country need to be embraced uniquely and managed effectively for business success. The payoff will always show in the long term results.

CHAPTER 11

Building your empire from Cents

A person I once cared for deeply said to me – Business is the most intimate of relationships one can ever have. He also said business plays a role in almost everything we do. I agree. Business is very much like life with everything that one goes through; from relationships, to bringing up children, to having fun at a club or park or even playing games; can be compared to or derived from a business lesson for possible improvement.

I watched a movie specifically because Brad Pitt was starring in it; but it was about a game that I do not really understand and to be quite frank, equate it to be as painful and boring to watch, as cricket., - Baseball.

The movie is based on the romance and love of the game of baseball and unquestionably the concept and context of the movie makes it hard not to see how romantic the game of baseball can be. The business aspect and perspective taken on the movie was undeniably genius and the storyline is a clear indication why baseball games have diehard fans and will keep paying for tickets and buying snacks in the millions just for this game. I too was hooked and surprisingly, find myself totally interested in the game today.

It's a Colombian Picture Production of the American League Division Series' Elimination Game in 2001 where the New York

Yankees are playing the Oakland Athletics (A's) and the first thing that catches my eye is 2 numbers carefully appearing on the screen with a black background – the upper one is $ 114, 457, 768 vs (the lower one) $ 39, 722, 689.

These numbers were the above mentioned teams budgets and they were facing each other in the final elimination. The A's lost the game – but their general manager (GM), who had also been a failed major league baseball player, and despite faring very poorly does not give up. So, keeps doing what he thought he knew best but for the first time decides he must separate himself from the rest.

He steals a young rookie from some other team, who has studied economics in Yale and has never played baseball before as his assistant general manager. The boy combines his love and knowledge of economics to completely turn the A's luck around and form a winning team based on a business and numbers point of view.

They have to build an unstoppable team with a very tight budget as compared to their competitors. They start using terms and a strategy never used before – building a team based strictly on their numerical base percentage.

Most players they pick are rejects from other teams, because of overlooked shortcomings, like looks, handicappers, injuries and baseless misconceptions from older or professional baseball scouts.

This newly created, financially broke, and looked down upon team faces opposition even from its own team scouts – particularly the more experienced folk who were still stuck in the known archaic methods of managing baseball.

When they embark on training; none of the GM's workmates or colleagues support him – in fact they make it so hard for him to work and blatantly ignore what he is trying to do – him and his newly appointed numeric employee are on their own.

Nonetheless, they do not give up.

This new strategy proves all other teams wrong in a few months – the A's go ahead and win 20 games in a row – the first of its kind winning streak in history. The doubting workmates and colleagues now start to believe.

The new strategy of working with numbers proved to the baseball league that much more can be done with much less – a very important business lesson. You can achieve quality and great results with very little but great planning.

It takes very little to go the extra mile, show competence, observe etiquette, look professional and garner respect. Training your staff adequately will clearly mean the difference between mediocrity and mastery.

Numbers can be used to calculate and predict a lot of wins in just about anything in your life. Thinking differently and setting yourself apart is key, and..,

If you do not adapt – you simply fade away.

CHAPTER 12

The Power of Humility in Business Success - Humility and Customer Service in Business

I had the pleasure of being invited to dinner by a good friend.

We went to a place called the "The Legend" in the Suburbs of Nairobi, Karen. We joined a group of Ladies and Gentlemen who were already there and the minute we walked in, we were greeted by warm smiles.

Formal introductions were made and the group, made us feel so welcome by engaging us in great jokes and good conversation. So much so, that I felt like I had known them for years.

We also had some talk on business and a very humble businessman shared very insightful knowledge on how successful business persons should humble themselves even to the younger generation. He said – you can be talking to a high school student and years later the student turns out to be a business person or even your boss.

Harold C Chase said – "The wise person possesses humility. He knows that his small island of knowledge is surrounded by a vast sea of the unknown"

From the onset – I could tell that the business owners were serious and passionate about their business. The place was well lit, it had good ambience and the waiters were friendly, on their toes and not wasting a single minute on any orders. The security officers too, were very well mannered and ushered sits for anyone they saw standing around the dance floor.

They had even thought of the chill that comes in Karen in the evening and had their outside cubicles fitted well, with clean clear plastic drapes that kept the cold out of the cubicles while maintaining the beauty of the restaurant. Not only is this a good idea to keep the customers there for a long time, but it is also good for ladies who like weaves to feel comfortable and not worry about adjusting seating positions lest the wind blows the hair to reveal underlines.

One of the humble gentlemen in our cubicle kept walking around and talking to guests at the place and at first, I thought – Oh! What a social person but later on found out that he was a partner of the premise.

This man's name is James Kimani and budding entrepreneurs can learn business sustainability tips from him.

For businesses to sustainably survive, keep their clients and attract even more – it is prudent for management or owners to have a humble rooting on the ground and know more about their clients. It is only from knowing your clients' needs that you can truly know if what you are offering is optimal.

Mr.Kimani and his friends got me thinking about Emotional Intelligence (EI) in Business.

Since the concept of EI was first introduced and the term burst to life in the mid-20th Century, it has been developed, adapted and embraced by the business world and more recently, by academics. EI skills have been strongly associated with dynamic leadership, satisfying personal life experiences and success in the workplace and thriving business management skills.

It's been proven that to be successful, one requires the effective awareness, control and management of one's own emotions, and those of other people, specifically ones you work with.

As a leader, one sets the emotional tone that others follow and how your business should be run. The emotional tone that permeates your organization starts with you as a leader and it depends highly on humility and EI.

The Legend, which is a great name for a business, lives up to its name and one, does not even have to meet the owners to understand how they take their business seriously.

The legend offers an array of services, from comfortable entertainment sitting, to private functions and can customize a function depending on a client's needs. I, for sure, know that I want to go back there with some of my friends.

The pleasure of meeting Mr. Kimani and his humble, but very wealthy friends was all my pleasure.

If management and businesses can learn a lesson or two from being humble, concentrating on their customer's needs, treating their workers with respect and understanding what emotional intelligence is – then the hardest battle of sustaining one's business has been won.

Using simple life lessons is key to maintaining a business and this will always show in the results.

Whenever I am depressed I tend to watch cartons as they instantly make me feel better.

I watched a wonderfully written and produced film called Ratatouille where an anthropomorphic rat aspires to be a master chef; with the underlying message being, geniuses can come from anywhere and we cannot afford to underestimate anyone.

Never the less, my favorite character held a cameo role as a food critique called Anton Ego - who gave a profound speech based on customer experience that go hand in hand with the power of humility coupled with great customer service.

Mr Ego, is generally, not so very popular. This is because he is a critique with very high standards and a negative critique from him can be heartbreaking, cause depression, and be career damaging or ego deflating. He is also not a very good looking man and is depicted with a skinny tall demeanor with puffy black eyes – but his word is as true and as pure as a lamb's skin. He only gives credit where it is due and never feels the need to lie on the quality of his food or what he partakes.

Bill Gates stated that "your most unhappy customers are your greatest source of learning" and according to Zig Ziglar – statistics suggest that when customers complain, business owners and managers ought to get excited about it. The complaining customer represents a huge opportunity for more business.

We as humans do not take criticism all too well, especially women; who ask for it all the time – but when presented with the naked truth they find it hard to swallow.

In business, complaining and criticizing customers, should be encouraged and invited – it is prudent for managers, customer service representatives and employees in general to be highly trained on the value of inviting constructive criticism and responding amicably with proven change to sustain the business. It is only from these complaining customers that one gets to truly know if the services you are offering are optimal.

Processes and manuals can be put in place on how to handle communication internally and externally but at some occasions some customers need to be let go of.

Creating a separate page on ones website for complaints and make sure that complaints are responded to within a reasonable time, create a complaint or feedback form but not the generic ones that tend to be a waste trees or paper, make sure your customer service lines are functional, test your customer service lines yourself with alternate numbers to make sure staff is working, make sure every complaint ticket is assigned a number and the representative attending to the complaint provides their full names for accountability purposes or paper thread incase the complaint needed immediate rectification.

The benefits of encouraging complaints and criticism are a myriad. It costs much more to attract a new customer than it does to maintain an existing one and research states shows that for every penny an organization spends on improved customer service, the returns can shoot from 30% to an amazing 400%

Comparing business to intimacy is unavoidable – Once you get a sexual partner and you do not like what they are doing, you can choose to share this at once with improved suggestions in order to maintain your relationship because you like each other or you can decide to pretend while complaining to friends outside or finding other avenues of satisfaction, but we all know the latter always ends up in a naught.

CHAPTER 13

Mixed Voices and the impact they can have on diversified business success with the Conundrum around Romance

I had the opportunity to lecture a development studies graduate course in the school of business in a privately owned campus in Nairobi. Surprisingly, all my students were female.

In the first class we discussed how we, as women can shape the future of our continent by exploring new and different ideas for development. The discussion was endless. We questioned our roles in leadership positions and discussed leading women in business especially in Africa and the hurdles women have had to overcome and still do in order to succeed.

Luckily, global advances have been made towards the recognition of the principle of women's political, economic and social equality. In Kenya, women continue to be marginalized in many areas of society, especially in the sphere of leadership, corporate management and integral decision making.

A few years ago a study carried out by the Kenya Institute of Management (KIM) sought to find out female representation in boards of state corporations and listed companies in Kenya. The findings revealed that state corporation boards comprised of 20% women and

80% men. Whereas in listed corporations only 12% of the board comprised of females. This study stated that among the listed companies only one had a female chairperson, and that women do not participate in policy making and influencing at public sector due to their limited numbers in the sector.

According to a 2009 survey by the Ministry of Gender, only 30.9% of those employed in Kenya's public service are women, 72% of who are in the lower cadres. This same inequity exists in the judiciary, in the leadership of political parties, and in political representation: Women hold only about 10 per cent of the seats in the 10th Parliament.

Interestingly women make 50% of the total Kenyan Population (acc 2009 national census). Ironically, Kenyan women have been at the forefront in championing the discourse and strategies that support women's rights and gender equality, politically, economically and socially–reinforced visibly by the 3rd World Conference of Women held in Nairobi in 1985;

Sadly, this pioneer spirit has not only failed in achieving effective political participation or the taking up of leadership positions in Kenya itself, but our women only served to nurture and observe the growth and success of women's movements in neighboring Rwanda, Uganda and Tanzania who now lead global statistics on women's representation in elective politics at 56.3, 31 and 30 per cent, respectively.

At the International inaugural Gender Equality Forum, businesses were frank in admitting that moving women into leadership roles was one of the greatest, and most intractable, challenges for workplace equality. Despite an increasingly robust business case for female leadership, women's representation at the top is stagnating, and in some cases shows signs of regressing.

Steering away from modest mechanisms to support women in the workplace now is the time for a radical approach to driving a step-change in women's representation.

Norway was the first country in the world to insist on female quotas for company boardrooms. In the last six years women's representation as leaders of Norwegian business has risen from 6% to 44%. In 2007, McKinsey and Catalyst's respective analyses made a significant contribution to the business case for women leaders. Both reports demonstrated a correlation between women's representation at board level and the financial performance of companies worldwide, pin-pointing a 30% turning point at which women's representation has a significant impact across a set of corporate performance indicators.

The United States proclaimed to be one of the most advanced nations in terms of women rights and liberalization cannot compare as well when it comes to how many women have held the topmost government positions till now. Within the U.S., female participation in political and business leadership has consistently stagnated around 18%. America still ranks 90th out of 186 worldwide in the Global political arena.

In 2010 women made up only 12.5% of the members of the corporate boards of FTSE 100 companies. This was up from 9.4% in 2004. Clearly this rate of increase is too slow.

The business case for increasing the number of women on corporate boards is clear. When women are so under-represented on corporate boards, companies are missing out, as they are unable to draw from the widest possible range of talent. Evidence suggests that organizations with a strong female representation at board and top management level perform better than those without and that gender-diverse boards have a positive impact on performance. It is clear that boards make better decisions where a range of voices, drawing on different life experiences, can be heard.

That mix of voices must include women. When you get to the level that you can have board members, this mix of voices will be evident simply in meetings and the results might depend on the kind of women you add to your board.

Having the mix of voices and a diversified employee pool can also create unwanted intimate feelings. If you run an organization or are running your business it might be very difficult for you to tell when employees are intimate – especially because you are busy looking at numbers and the organizational running of your company.

As I grow older I realize that it is much better to work in a place with no office romance as the drama that follows when one is in love is almost uncontrollable.

Love is the only thing that can turn an animal into a coward, the emotion that stands out and cannot be hidden no matter what you try.

An emotion that cannot be controlled and has no boundaries what so ever. Love can be granted as a reward and one can invite it – but it almost impossible to turn it off

Love cannot be bought – all other things pertaining sexual encounters with whips, fingers, mouths or just plain intercourse are all for sale – but the one thing that cannot be bought no matter what, is true love. The wonderfully acted movie – Indecent Proposal is a good example of what love can and cannot do.

Love can motivate people to enormous journeys and push them to see things they had previously thought were impossible. That feeling one gets when they are around someone they feel totally comfortable with cannot be compared to any material gift. The sweating, the speechlessness the shakes are all involuntary. Love is the one emotion that can make one go crazy and without it one can simply wither away and die.

On the other hand Love can confuse one into a state of no comprehensive understanding and it is because of how powerful this feeling is that Love in itself has started wars all over the world.

Now, when you get this in the work place, especially in your business and the relationship does not end up in a solid marriage it can really disrupt work flow and performance.

It will be very hard to keep the relationship under the radar as it is obvious when two people have feelings for each other. It gets trickier when the two handling the office romance are good employees – the organization might be looking at losing two good workers.

Understanding that company policy of not having affairs is only put in place to protect the companies integrity and maintain a nice working environment.

One can have discreet sexual encounters but make sure that they remain just that – discreet. And if you like someone else and cannot live with the lie – say sorry and look for ways to start something else or move on.

Mixing love, business and work is not a good recipe and it can get really messy. Some people might take advantage of the feeling and take it to another bad level by trying to use one for monetary gain or slander.

Love and office romance contribute to a huge percentage of the number of sexual harassment law suits that have been recorded by the Equal Employment Opportunity Commission in America and to curb this, most organizations and companies are strict on the no romance policy in the workplace.

Should it get to the part where you absolutely cannot live without your colleague then lay out some rules between the two of you that you will keep in the closet for as long as you work there.

See each other way past office hours; do not have the same time schedules, be as discreet as possible, unless off course you plan on getting married.

Remember office gossip gets juicier once people know that some individuals are carrying out a romance and it can get out of hand when employees sit at lunch time to discuss other employees. It is bad for business and is very bad for employee morale.

According to ITV.com, "what is love" was the most searched phrase in Google in 2012 – and if this is true, then it just goes to show how many are confused from Love itself. I know I am completely scared of it – so if you do not mind being called a robot at work but do your job well – then keep off the office romance – it begs more disadvantages than it does advantages. You would rather keep off the drama, than invite it. I call that self-preservation

CHAPTER 14

Right Networks for Business Success

When I was young I remember my dad used to get really irritated by some friends I had chosen to hang out with. He would vehemently tell me not to keep some friends and as a child, I did not understand and would get angry and question why he would tell me not to mingle with certain individuals.

As I have grown older, it is evident that he had my best interest at heart and he was right. I could have been too stubborn to see or too young to understand – but the truth is, even in Business when one surrounds themselves with bad business persons it can result in hurting your business and subsequently your business network.

The power that peer pressure has can go unnoticed at the early stages but the consequences can be very dire and harm one's good morals into a downward spiral. This power can happen to anyone, young or old.

Sometimes we surround ourselves with certain individuals and after some time we realize that the individuals are not straight people or their thinking, is way different than ours. But because we feel lonely or want to be accepted in society we keep that company. Be it of a close friend, or relative or an older person we once looked up to.

What we do not realize or are in denial to accept is that our own good moral is being hurt much more than the other person who might be a seasoned individual and has chosen to follow a life of questionable standards or different moral ethic.

I have recently started reading the bible and the verses on keeping good company are many both in the old and new testaments. Some of my favorites being: - 1 Corinthians 15:33 "Do not be misled; Bad company corrupts good character". Psalms 26: 4-5 "I do not sit with men of falsehood, nor do I consort with hypocrites. I hate the assembly of evildoers, and I will not sit with the wicked."

Proverbs 14:7 "Leave the presence of a fool, for there you do not meet words of Knowledge" and Proverbs 22: 24-25 "Make no friendship with a man given to anger, nor go with a wrathful man, lest you learn his ways and entangle yourself in a snare"

This is not only true for character building but it is also true if you want to achieve business success.

When one chooses to engage or follow a business network, they are hoping to be linked to groups of like-minded business persons who can appreciate, recognize, and think creatively to achieve business success.

If one is in the farming business, then one should seek professional successful farmers who will guide him into achieving greater results via good consultation and social talks.

Technology has revolutionized how business networks are built and nowadays networks can be on a plethora of social platforms. Although these are great platforms to meet likeminded thinkers, it is always a great idea if you are in the same area to have a face-to-face meeting when you decide to indulge or pursue a business relationship.

But picking the right network is, key. Just like friendship and personal relationships, if one surrounds themselves with bad company, chances are they will fall harder without realizing it up until it is too late to pick yourself up with dignity after having lost your moral or good character.

In a traditional world it is harder for women to have wider or broader business networks as men do, as they tend to have personal inhibitions and can be prone to following the wrong networks without seeing or noticing that they should change their networking approach.

Creating networks of men especially for women can get a tad bit tricky. It gets even harder when the women are single. It is simpler for a married woman to increase her network of men as she will get good contacts from her spouse. Single women have to work a little harder to get trusted networks and it takes a longer time. But the secret is to be persistent and keep knocking on doors until you find the right persons to work with.

Choosing friends should be the same when choosing business relations and associates. You have to choose wisely for better moral ethic and sustainable results.

CHAPTER 15

Choosing the right management style at the right time

Meet Johnson: – a proud business man who owns a number of businesses but his pride and joy is a 3 storey restaurant in the suburbs of an affluent East African area. The restaurant is strategically situated and as such gets quite the customers. Customer service is not top notch, the place is not always as clean as it should be, but the ambience (space wise) of the restaurant and its location attracts a good number of clients to keep it open.

Johnson runs the business solo and with an iron fist – he manages the place with complete authority and no one else can question his decisions. He controls the team, making decisions and running operations without seeking or considering input from his direct reports. According to Johnson, his employees are just a replaceable resource and not the core of the organization. He preaches and believes in top-down communication, wherein orders are given by the higher hierarchical level to the lower ones. Johnson seldom lets others make decisions, he feels most qualified and experienced, considers his views to be most valid, lacks confidence in others abilities, is very critical of differing opinions, rarely gives recognition, is easily offended, uses others for his benefit, is action oriented, and highly competitive. The concept of "employee satisfaction" does not hold importance for Johnson.

This kind of Management is called the Autocratic or Authoritarian management style - it is also known as totalitarianism or dictatorship. It does forge an atmosphere of discipline in the organization; however, it will inevitably cause dissatisfaction and a lack of "creative space" for the employees.

Because of this Management style – workers hardly stay more than 6 months. Absenteeism and the rate of turnover, is very high for comfort and employees do not feel valued. Sadly, because the rate of unemployment is so high in Kenya – Johnson will always find new employees. Hardworking, humble Kenyans who need to feed their children and put food on their tables. The domino effect is that the business might never reach its optimum output in terms of gross profit and growth. The amount spent hiring new inexperienced workers, training them and then losing them in a split second, does take a toll on the business. This poor management style easily undermines the business and fails to recognize its own mistakes. The biggest strength of this style is to produce action when it is needed.

Meet Macy – an entrepreneur and business woman who owns and runs a bakery. Macy and Johnson are both in the food industry. The authority of running the bakery is in Macy's hand only, however, she cares more about the employees than outcomes and profits. She is more like a parent than a boss to her employees. Her employees are the heart of the organization. She believes in top-down as well as bottom-up communication.

The complete authority lies in the hands of one individual; however the method of functioning is very different as compared to Autocratic. Macy's management style is called Paternalistic. This style used by Macy encourages input and feedback from her direct reports and bases her decisions at least in part on their views. Her workers feel valued because their opinions matter. The entire team takes ownership of a project because of each team member's individual contributions.

Paternalistic management is also very dictatorial, but includes the best interests of the employees as well as the business itself. In a very basic sense, the leader is often in a better situation to make overall organizational decisions due to experience. Managers practicing this style care about the social needs of their employees (for example, being happy), but it also slows down and clouds the decision-making process

Consequently Macy has retained the same manager for the last 3 years. Her workers seem to love coming to work and give more than they are asked for. Her business is growing, slowly, but surely and steadily.

Both Johnson and Macy are running their businesses the way they know how — they might be unaware of the management styles they are practicing, which could be closely linked to their individual personality and leadership qualities or based on the principles they each follow.

While paternalistic management is the proven and preferred style in business, autocratic management can still function effectively. The workforce may dispute this fact, as they tend to be generally uninterested in their jobs and may be mistrustful of management. Yet, if you are part of an autocratic management group, you can still use teams profitably and improve the morale of your staff if you do it wisely.

There are different management styles that you can choose when running your business — it all depends on the results you want to achieve. One single management style cannot be used for an entire organization all the time. Managing a group of individuals is almost like baby-sitting different children, attention is sometimes given to each, but when results are required almost immediately and are varying, then the management style needs to change.

When you get to stage where you can employ and need to manage your staff — it would be worth the while to research different management styles so that you can determine what style you will use and for what gain.

Managing is not for all - but can be learnt and almost perfected the results in this case will show in the long and short term goals of your venture.

CHAPTER 16

Planning With Simple Budgeting Tools

The importance of planning for anything can never be over emphasized. Without proper planning your venture or business idea might be tougher than you imagined and harder to start seeing good profit margins. Even in the event of winning a lottery – without planning on how you will use your money might mean the same as not winning the money in the first place. It might fly right past your fingers without your knowledge.

Whatever your business is - from selling doughnuts, used cars dealer, cleaning floors to working as a CEO; you all have a business thing in common; you work with and are governed by a budget.

A budget simply put is a money plan.

There are two basic approaches or philosophies when it comes to budgeting. One approach focuses on mathematical models, and the other on people.

The first school of thought believes that financial models, if properly constructed, can be used to predict the future. The focus is on variables, inputs and outputs, drivers and the like. The other school of thought holds that it's not about models, it's about people. No matter how sophisticated models can get, the best information comes from the people in the business.

I will share with you my top budgeting tools that can be used in any business to help you determine whether you have enough money to fund operations, expand the business and generate income. These tools are better utilized with clearly defined templates created to fit your organization – one generic template, might not work for various organizations. It's critical to use models that address individual business goals.

Revenue Projection Model: This model is used to forecast business revenues under different conditions and is a great way to start your budgeting process. Your budget should reflect the anticipated currency value of sales and services. This Model provides a comprehensive Excel forecasting tool that analyzes and manipulates the price, quantity, and percentage increase to give different possible outcomes.

Sales Forecasting Guide: If you have several revenue streams, your budget should include anticipated income from each of them. It should also predict future sales based on past performance. Categorizing each stream allows you to identify which parts of your business are profitable and which are not. If your business is a start-up, you may not be familiar with creating a sales forecast.

Sales Plan Template: Once you have a sales forecast in place you can use the Sales Plan Template to implement the forecast. The Template might include descriptions for the necessary sections: sales targets, market potential, sales strategy, execution details, budget, sales force compensation, sales force training and a time-line for execution.

Capital Budgeting Analysis: This tool helps you figure out how much money you need to put in place for new equipment or procedures to launch new products or increase production or services. The Excel spreadsheet model you create allows you to organize different project metrics, such as payback period, profitability index, internal rate of return, and net present value. This budget estimates the value of capital purchases your business needs to grow and increase revenues. If your business involves jobs or projects, budgeting will probably include aspects of both product and service revenue budgeting.

Cash Flow Forecast: A cash flow budget details the amount of cash you collect and pay out. This is generally tallied on a monthly basis and you track your sales and other receivables from income sources and contrast them against how much you pay to suppliers and in expenses.

You can use this to predict annual profits versus end-of-year debt. Most importantly this sheet provides a guide for tracking which arms of your business are most profitable, and show which creditors are owed various amounts of the company's future profits.

Expense Budget: After you figure out how much you are making, you can determine how much you can spend. This is a spreadsheet used to track expenses throughout the calendar year. The Expense Budget lists the most common expense categories and allows you to enter monthly totals, which are then added for an annual total and a monthly average.

Asset Depreciation Calculator and Schedule: A tool ignored by many, while in essence, many of the assets you've purchased for your business like, vehicles, machinery, and computers – have a finite life. This tool helps you calculate the depreciation expense for all your assets and it would be prudent to factor this expense into your budget.

12 Month Profit and Loss Projection Model: This helps to predict sales and cost for the whole year, not like a detailed financial statement but as a guide to help forecast profits and losses for up to 12 months.

Unquestionably, planning for the future is an essential piece to the survival of your business. As the wise man says "Fail to Plan or Plan to Fail"

The payoff of planning for anything you want to do will always show in the results.

CHAPTER 17

Learning from failure, Destroying to Construct or Ripping off that rearview mirror

A very young aspiring farmer in Kenya, East Africa is almost giving up on his dream to make some profit from an honest living. He has an acre of land and has grown pineapples. The Pineapples are doing well but his neighbors' and uninvited guests seem to be enjoying the fruits of his labor.

They are stealing his fruit.

This is an obstacle that he had not envisioned or planned for when he set out to grow his cash crop. An obstacle that has crippled him, to conclude, that he cannot keep growing pineapples.

He is somewhat lucky as he is young and can afford to make mistakes before he finally realizes how to make a sustainable profit. But with business, one has to be mentally prepared for pitfalls and challenges that might even make one close up shop and have to go back to the drawing board to create ways of starting a new.

Getting up after a major shake or fall and making it is the true way to success. All business persons must understand that one has to fail a number of times to effectively make it in business.

Business Women take falling slightly differently as compared to business men when they fall. Women tend to take their failure much more personally, internalize it, take a little more time to recover and sometimes even give up on their pursuit to financial happiness and independence.

A study done by the Global Entrepreneurship fund and Babson College revealed that women had lower perception capabilities, self-esteem and confidence than men when endeavoring to establish and run a business.

Women also tend to over analyze issues and end up thinking too much about the possibility of failure that it takes longer for them to actually start a business; and when they fall – getting back up is much harder.

Once business people realize that you cannot pursue something that is going to effectively work well and fall in place over night, then, half the battle of succeeding has been won.

Failures are never the end. In fact, failure can be a way of getting back to the drawing board and thinking up new creative ways of starting a new. Failures must be expected when starting a new venture, but expecting and accepting failure are two disparate things.

Many do not accept failure that easy and some do not even understand what they are going through; a good support system, individual focus and motivation must prevail and the notion that you cannot just give up after your first failure. Overcoming and conquering your fear should be the first step. Knowing what your fears are, understanding them, dealing with them and moving on with a clearer picture, is key.

A lot of time can be wasted thinking about why you failed and why it did not work; but its working and doing the business that ends the failing procrastination. Get up, dust yourself off and try again – but with a much better understanding.

There are many reasons that startups or businesses fail and some entrepreneurs could be in denial when dealing with their own ideas and concepts. Before you get up again, try and focus and write a list of what went wrong so you may not plunge into the same hole again.

Pick the right team, get professional advice, try separate yourself from the rest - in order to achieve your own niche, do not get stuck on your original idea (chances are, if you failed the idea might not have been well executed), do not spend too much money – most people think that having a lot of money is fundamental in doing business; that, is but a fallacy – you can make much out of very little.

Feeling jaded should be the last option for an entrepreneur or business person. Self-confidence too, plays an important role in making it after a fall.

Confident business men and women feel competent from the inside out. They use their knowledge and talents to genuinely try to be useful and succeed at hand. Truth is, to succeed in business – having Self-Confidence is vital. Most successful business men and women have some level of confidence; yet there are days, minutes, hours or weeks in the business person's life when they are unsure of how to tackle some business challenges- everyone at one time goes through these shaky times – but the trick is to stay on track and not let a trying time hold you back to achieving business success.

Learning how to overcome bouts of self-doubt can only come from within. One must be completely honest with themselves by assessing ones' ability and deficiencies and then getting comfortable enough to work on them and assertively correct them. You have to practice doing things that you have not done before and could be unsure of and embracing new opportunities to prove to yourself and others that you can confront and work on difficult things.

One important factor to always remember is that your confidence must bear exemplary and evident results – one must be able to deliver on their confidence making sure it's quality, memorable and sustainable results.

Lastly – never give up; push as much as you can within your capability and sit back to watch your hard work come into play.

Within the first few months of Obama's Inauguration, he introduced a stimulus package for Americans to deal with the then tough economic situation. My friend got a cheque and added this to her tax returns with some help from friends and family that helped her cover some bills and renovate part of her kitchen that was in desperate need of attention.

She tore down a part of her wall got affordable building material did most of the easy stuff herself but got a friend to help her with the construction work.

In about a month and a half her kitchen looked totally different and surprisingly spacious.

Another friend of mine had thought of himself as an athlete to reckon with from his weekly workouts, so, he decided to sign up for some Kick Boxing classes. He was not a smoker, drunk socially and was an avid gym user. When he went in for the first class he came back and explained how frustrated he was at the tutor for asking him to start on exercises and a training routine he was sure he could do in his sleep. Nevertheless, he went back, but still, this 'simple' training went on for quite a while.

Three months later – he came back with a completely different outlook on his perceived simple training.

My ex- Husband who was studying Physics was very handy with his hands and loved working on cars. I took out our first car for a long drive to see some friends and I must have driven too fast or did not handle the gear box too well nor the clutch because on my way back home there was a clicking sound in the hood of the car, it kept jerking around and the rumbling noise was so loud that I could be heard miles away. In short - I had broken the axle of the car.

He took this surprisingly well but let me know that we would either have to rent a car or I would have to walk to work. Since I can be very frugal, I opted for the latter as I thought to myself it would only take a few hours to fix. When I got back home from work – the entire engine of the car was literally sprawled in our drive way, nuts and bolts all over, with jars of oil and a rather large tool box.

The common denominator with these three scenarios is that destruction and construction share two sides of the same coin.

Sometimes in life and in business one must destroy or break down something in order to rebuild a new better looking or working version.

The Kitchen did not take much money but a considerate amount of hard work; had she not torn down part of her kitchen the result would not have been the same.

The kickboxing enthusiast thought he knew it all but the instructor had to take him way back to the very basic simple start and break his self-imposed ego in order to see a great kick boxer with trained discipline.

If my man had not taken the engine apart to change the axles, our car might have never lasted us long after that mishap and we would have probably been looking at more damage or even buying a new car.

In Business when one decides to take a different approach especially during the self-actualizing and growing phase, it can be helpful to tear down what you thought you had in order to see a new and better beginning or greater results. This is true in life as well, sometimes we live in a certain way, we are so sure is right, up until we meet someone or encounter various things in life that make us question our previous ways of living or practicing our businesses.

Taking apart or destroying to rebuild is not an easy task it is just like accepting change (everybody wants change but no one is willing to change) – but, it is imperative for the growth and sustainability of your business and personal life. Endings could be disguised beginnings which we do not realize when we are so stuck in what we are used to that it requires mental preparation to adopt.

Before you make that change, believe, strategize, make a simple budget, be specific and tabulate it as a timeline in your life.

The rewards of embracing the two sides of the coin will only show in the long term results while you quietly meditate on Socrates quote "The secret of change is to focus all of your energy, not on fighting the old, but on building the new.

I have very many brothers but I only trust a few. For example, one is in Europe and the other one is in America. They are both very hard workers and know much about planning and operating a business – infact, most of my rudimentary business lessons have been learnt from them. They both imagine solutions and or invent fresh approaches that leave me amazingly surprised as to how I never imagined that would work before.

They are both similar in many ways but very different in others. One of them is very patient talks with a soft tone and does not rush into anything. The other, is not that patient, works on many different projects at a time and when he speaks, he speaks with a somewhat commanding tone. Both are entrepreneurs but one works on expanding a single concept while the other works on various ideas at a time.

I have always wondered why the seemingly serial entrepreneur would work so hard on a project and after many years of toil and evident projected future sustainability, just get up and leave without a single tear nor regret and never look back; yet go out and start right over with yet another tasking venture. I was convinced he does not care about himself and generally does not care about anyone else nor keeping a profitable business – but I was wrong.

He has understood and fully embraced the term ripping off the rear view mirror for his life and business ventures. The business world is like life as a whole -- it never stands still and change is inevitable. Sometimes that change is for the better and sometimes businesses fall short of good know how or the knowledge of surviving around change.

Many a time when driving, we focus so much on the rear view mirror that we forget to keep moving or get distracted with what is in our wake. The term ripping off the rear view mirror means, having no desire to look at your past, not wasting too much of your time or energy wondering what is coming for you from your past – simply moving forward no matter what.

Most east African financial years end in December – meaning if your accounting has been done well, by January, you know where your business is and where it is headed. If it's good or bad; if the latter is the case and you have ignored all the signs of your business falling apart – ripping off the rear-view mirror might be the solution for you.

Successful entrepreneurs can tell you stories or two of how they have had to sell their businesses and moved on to better ventures. Sometimes you have to let go of a bad (loss) or even good (profit) thing for projected higher successes. Changing a business model or service can be a way to save your business too.

There is so much business opportunity out there just waiting to be explored; while some business owners' painfully hold on to what they know is not going to reap results or is simply killing them as human beings. The power of deciding to get rid of the rear-view mirror and assertively, carefully but steadily keep going can be pure bliss.

But deciding to rip off that rear-view mirror should be done with confidence and great skill – one should seriously think about what they want to accomplish, the consequences of not looking back and embracing the journey forward with expectations of many ups and downs but a clear goal and focus. One should also come to terms and have a good understanding of who they truly are. Truth is, if you were once a good businessman and made a profit, then chances of repeatable entrepreneurial success are imminent.

Embrace the idea of ripping off that rear-view mirror with focus of what lies ahead.

CHAPTER 18

Importance of Options, Imagination and Creativity rather than stressed upon Education

So you wake up one morning and as you're taking your morning coffee, or enjoying great Kenyan Coffee or South African tea, a great voice speaks to you and says – I will grant your life's desires now but you have to choose between two things offered.

What are the choices you ask with excitement?

The first is tangible, is most people's dream but the second is not and you really cannot feel it. What are the choices you remark, once more? The first is a sack full of money and the second is great business options. What would you choose?

A colleague and I were discussing this over lunch a few months ago. Fact – whatever business you are in - businesses require money for working capital and to invest for future growth; interestingly most people believe that in order to start a business you need to have a boat load of money and everything else will fall in place for the business to succeed.

Options on the other hand are priceless. It is very hard to place real value on having great business options. Let me share examples of businesses that exist solely from consumer and or business options

Local hairdresser – my neighborhood has more than 4 hairdressing salons each with more than 3 full time employees. The prices of their services differs a little but the work is pretty much almost the same – these hairdressers are still in business and rely on the fact that the consumers will come back based on the differentiated product or stylist that will suit each individual.

Airlines – yes, there are a number but I will mostly always fly emirates, or Qatar because of the service I have come accustomed to over the years and their prices are good for my pocket. Airlines provide options for the consumer to make a decision on which they will fly.

Retail supermarkets - they all almost sell the same products but differentiate themselves by offering more options to the consumers hence the creation of one stop markets.

In today's business world it is almost impossible to re-invent the wheel – successful businessmen are simply re-designing the wheel with creativity and added value.

Option can be used instead of equity to effectively maximize returns while reducing risk. Investors and traders can use options to diversify their portfolios, increase returns without even purchasing underlying securities.

No matter how you look at it – there is power in Options and it lies in versatility. You can adapt or adjust your business position according to any situation that arises. You can be as speculative, creative and as conservative as you want; You can do anything that will ensure successful business growth with options.

Startups that show signs of failure can be dissolved at once to provide room for better and more sustainable options.

So when that magic genie appears and you choose the 'money instead of the box'– you should hope that you have been well educated or can afford to educate yourself on sustainable business options and can get access to them.

Business persons and businesses should explore practical ways to foster encouragement of options and increase profitability. Working with seasoned industries and associations and learning from experienced successful models to ensure quality sustainable options will be evident in ventures' results.

CHAPTER 19

It is never too late to have a smile on your face

One of my favorite classes is a core entrepreneurial class for both graduate and undergraduate students. I usually take the first lesson to get to know the students and understand why they are there and whether they are merely taking the class to satisfy the core requirements or are interested in what the class will offer to a budding entrepreneurial mind.

A class that stood out for me in these Entrepreneurship Skills classes was a mixture of young and old students. The oldest being 65 and the youngest 20; it was such a diverse class that I actually looked forward to lecturing it and sometimes went over the allocated 3 hours just to listen to the students differing points of view.

Their first assignment was to write a 2 page business plan of their choice and stick to the basics. They were also supposed to analyze themselves according to their age and briefly explain why their chosen businesses would flourish. One of the younger students presented hers with total confidence stating that all her employees, especially ones in management would be less than 30 years of age and if she had to employ anyone past 40 – they would only be drivers as they are too old and accomplish tasks way too slowly. She was convinced that when one is past 40 – they are not capable of recognizing opportunity and do not think proactively.

I immediately differed.

An entrepreneur is a person who recognizes an opportunity, creatively fills a gap, assumes risk, manages the business and realizes profit.

It really does not matter how old you are – for some, that need arises earlier in life and for some a little later. It depends on an individual and their environment.

Some of the most successful businesses have been founded by persons past 35.

There are advantages of founding a business when one is young; the energy, curiosity, room to make ample mistakes and learning from the mistakes. Similarly an older or late booming entrepreneur has a probably sounder mind, s/he knows exactly what they want and work towards a specific more mature goal.

The founder of FORD Motor, Henry Ford created his highly successful company just before his 40th Birthday.

The famous Kentucky Fried Chicken (KFC) that is outstandingly successful in Kenya and some parts of Africa was founded by Colonel Sanders who never gave up at the age of 66 after a new highway almost ran him out of business by driving traffic away from his business premise.

The founder and CEO of Denali flavors – a Michigan based ice cream company started it when he was 71.

The former basketball superstar and one of my life heroes – Michael Jordan took his chance on business when he was 49. He has a steakhouse in New York, 2 additional restaurants in Chicago, a car dealership in Durham and a motorcycle race team. Although his talent and game gave him an advantage, he was still a late bloomer in the entrepreneurial world of business. Michael Jordan's fan and Americas Media Proprietor – Oprah Winfrey was also a late bloomer in the world of Business.

Franny Martin started her 'cookies on call' business after working for years in the corporate world, when she was 56 from doing what she loved most – cookie-baking.

African late blooming and highly successful entrepreneurs include the likes of Chris Kirubi, Susan Mashibe, founder & CEO of Tanjet,

Youssef Mansour, Tabitha Mukami Muigai – Karanja, Founder & CEO of Keroche Breweries, Jim Ovia, Founder of Zenith Bank Group, Naushad Merali who launched Kencell, and Moulay Hafid Elalamy founder of Group Saham among others.

Age is really nothing but a number – when one decides their chance at stepping out and following their entrepreneurial business calling - the energy and focus one puts into their dreams will always show in the results.

Counting numbers as profit is not the same as counting the number of birthdays.

While achieving this dream you have to keep in mind one simple but powerful facial factor – a smile.

I regarded myself as a very happy person for a really long time. I was always smiling and laughing; in fact in one Organizational Behavior class the Lecturer asked what our biggest weaknesses were, and I was sure it was how happy and nice I was.

That started to change when I realized being too trusting and nice to everyone was a killer instead of a builder. It is almost impossible for everyone to like you and it is even worse when you continue being nice when the results only seem to be detrimental and you keep having sleepless nights; not because you have done wrong - but because every time you do right, there is an equal and opposite reaction.

I therefore made a conscious effort to break bad, keep my solitude and pushed a lot of people away to try and change the niceness. The one thing that kept constant was that I was still a happy person inside and I could not change what I was.

My change was and still is a challenge, it is not easy to embrace change at all, especially when you have become comfortable with the existing environment and do not know what to expect after the change has begun. Although, you know that change is inevitable, complete comprehension comes with a plethora of challenging battles.

The secret is to keep a smile at all times while still being tough and maintaining the integrity of the path you have chosen to follow.

This is especially true for people living in the business world. That world is tough and the stumbling blocks can be very shaky – but imagine giving a presentation in tears and see just how far that presentation will go.

The unfortunate thing about this world is that there are good people and bad people – the problems going around in the world from the economy to unnatural and natural disasters has seen bad people multiply by the numbers and come from anywhere – some people are genuinely happy for others when they are blessed with good things, like, success, good grades, hard work, integrity or even having a wonderful family – but some people do not like seeing others move faster or be more successful than them and that is just very sad.

When, one decides to venture into a business they must understand that they will be facing good people, bad people and the inevitable obstacles of business success – but the secret is to keep a smile no matter what you are going through; Because, no matter where you go and where you are, a smile is worth nothing but the results are immediate and sometimes everlasting.

When you smile the world smiles back at you – you can keep your integrity in the office or at your place of business, but when you keep this with a frown all the time – the effects trickle down like a domino effect to your employees, business partners and eventually your entire organization, it might even go all the way to your home.

It gets very tricky when you start consciously harming someone for no reason and even trickier when you harm someone because of your grumpiness or sore thumb, this, can also deeply affect the person you are and make you into a completely unhappy person and the world is not good when you decide to take this path – it can only lead to a downward spiral that can go down many generations in your family or organization - a very hard battle to fight with the world and mother nature.

It is strange when things do not seem like they are going well, one starts thinking of all the things they should have done years ago and regret seems to be the best blanket to cozy up to – that is a bad path to take – regret never helped anyone and it is a waste of time crying over spilt milk – so, do not give up and just keep going – but keep going with a smile on your face.

The smile and your unbreakable motivation will only show in the results, and you will be smiling inwardly when you attain your goal and target.

CHAPTER 20

Business Principles Derived from Nature always spell success

Nature is simply breathtaking; True genius of what Man, with all his knowledge and brains can never achieve. Everything in nature is there for a reason, nothing was put there by mistake and that is why our maker will always be referred to as God, All Powerful, Omnipresent and Almighty among other adorning words. This is because – there is no single mistake in what he/she made. Nature's creation is just, perfect.

While working in the Capitol City of California – Sacramento, a great friend of mine called Richard introduced me to the art of feeding and watching adorable wild animals. During my lunch hour, I would go to the park with a bag of peanuts to feed the squirrels. Richard had worked for the Government longer than I had and was quite resourceful – from his educative talks, his taste for fine dining, his thirst for knowledge on a daily basis and his endless questions towards nature and business.

Feeding the squirrels, at first to me was like watching paint dry, but, by my third feed – I got so addicted I begun going there on Saturdays and Sundays. It is simply amazing what I learnt from these little creatures.

Squirrels, just like dogs bury their bones, will bury their food. They would cleverly look around prior to coming for a nut as if checking to see if their friends have seen the peanut they are after, come pick it, sniff on it, feel on it with both their paws and hide the food in a different place every time. They would not tire at all and the more peanuts I threw out there – the faster they would work towards their storage and acquiring food goal.

Another animal that fascinated me to watch was the African Dung Rolling beetle – I spent a lot of time in Machakos County, Kenya, last year and since I could not afford to throw peanuts for the squirrel folk – I spent time with the cows. The African dung beetle will start with nothing of cow dung and literally walk backwards gathering dung to go and hide in some burrow far away from the initial pick up point.

If we as humans took life lessons from nature we would achieve objectives far beyond our wildest human imagination. Nature is there to be enjoyed, nurtured and provides for us the basic necessities we need for survival – understanding it and giving it the credit it so deserves will only make us better and closer to its maker.

Business wise if we took a lesson from these little creatures called squirrels; we would learn an important lesson on saving for a rainy day. Seeing and recognizing there is an investment, looking around and seeing whom among your network is interested in that venture, holding hands, analyzing the investment and finally safekeeping it for a better tomorrow; knowing very well, it will not happen overnight, but the more you save, the more you can predict your business success and achieve the goal you are aspiring.

Squirrels are credited with helping forest health by spreading some form of fungi that helps trees grow. We would take this lesson and give back to our environment through community service and creating projects that aim at restoring our environment.

If we could take lessons from the African Dung beetle, we would know that you can make a thriving business out of collecting waste and the undervalued importance of recycling. Not only do these beetles work all day to bury that dung, but what they do helps the environment by stopping flies from breeding in the dung areas subsequently releasing the dung's nutrients into the soil and make fertilizer wherever they go.

They also eat this dung, use it as their homes and the mother beetle lays her eggs in the dung and when they hatch the young feed on the same dung.

Lessons to learn are; if one is persistent and resilient on whatever it is they do to make a profit and do it well it will always succeed. People may look down at the business you might be doing, whether it is collecting waste or not – but getting your hands dirty while keeping your eye on the bigger price will show in the long term results.

Nature is the greatest and most endless source of learning and human improvement, businessmen and women might want to observe nature closely to realize unimaginable business success.

www.ingramcontent.com/pod-product-compliance
Lightning Source LLC
Chambersburg PA
CBHW031537210526
45464CB00003B/1053